Breaking Free: A Journey from Chaos to Clarity

By Nicky Re

Copyright © 2025 Nicky Re.

All rights reserved.

No part of this publication may be reproduced, distributed, or transmitted in any form or by any means, including photocopying, recording, or other electronic or mechanical methods, without the prior written permission of the author, except in the case of brief quotations used in reviews or critical articles.

This is a work of nonfiction based on real experiences.

Cover design by the author.

Published by Infinite Light Publishing

ISBN: 978-1-0369-1583-4

First Edition: 2025

Printed in the United Kingdom

For enquiries, contact: hello@breakingfreebook.com

www.breakingfreebook.com

Dedication

For Amber.

The woman who never gave up on me.

You stood by me during my most challenging moments.

You never tried to fix me—you just loved me through it.

This book is ours.

And to you, the reader—

The version of you that almost gave up.

This is proof that you didn't.

You held on. You're still here.

And that means everything.

Author's Note

If you picked up this book because you're in pain, feeling stuck, or searching for a lifeline—it just might be the best decision you've made in years.

You need to know that you're not alone on this journey, and what you're about to read isn't just my story—it's yours too.

This is the book I wish someone had handed me years ago. I didn't need a condescending diatribe full of motivational buzzwords, I needed truth. I needed someone to say, "I feel that way too", and show me the way out.

That's what this book does, and like life, it may appear messy. It's raw. It's honest. But most importantly—it's real.

I wrote it from the edge, and now I'm handing it to you, from the other side.

You've got this. You already hold the key.

Now let's break free.

– Nicky

Trigger Warning & Disclaimer

This book contains candid, unfiltered accounts of deeply personal experiences, including discussions of mental health struggles, emotional breakdowns, trauma, and self-destructive behaviours. Some passages may be triggering for readers who have faced similar challenges.

The language in this book reflects the authenticity of the journey—including moments of strong emotions and profanity. Nothing has been softened or censored. This is not a story that can be told with half-truths. It is hard-hitting, intense, and deeply real—but that is often what we most need to hear.

If you are currently struggling, please read with care and take breaks when needed. If you find yourself affected by any of the content, know that you are not alone. Support is available.

This book is not intended as a substitute for professional help. It is a personal journey of transformation, survival, and breaking free from destructive cycles. Please seek the guidance of a qualified mental health professional if needed.

Above all, this book exists to show you one thing: change is possible. No matter how lost you feel, there is always a way forward.

Table of Contents

Dedication	2
Author's Note	3
Trigger Warning & Disclaimer	4
Introduction	**10**
Why This Book Exists & Who It's For	10
Why I'm the One Writing This Book	11
What You'll Get from This Book	12
Chapter 1: The Breaking Point	**14**
Chapter 2: Echoes of Early Years – Unpacking Your Foundations	**20**
Questions to Reflect On:	21
Trying to Belong	21
Questions to Reflect On:	22
Becoming the Showman	22
Questions to Reflect On:	23
Living Between Two Worlds	23
Questions to Reflect On:	24
Growing Up Sensitive	24
Questions to Reflect On:	25
Looking Back with Clarity and Compassion	25
Final Questions to Reflect On:	26
Insight	26
Chapter 3: Slipping Into the Cycle	**28**
The Early Signs—Feeling the Pull	29
The Cycle Tightens Its Grip	31
Questions to Reflect On:	32
The Emotional Aftermath—The Shame Spiral	33
The Moment the Mask Slipped	34
The Inner Conflict—Knowing but Ignoring	35
Questions to Reflect On:	36
The Role of Others—Enablers and Eye-Openers	36

The Breaking Point (Before the Breakdown)	37
Final Thoughts—Standing at the Edge	38
Your Turn—Reflect, Write, Reclaim	38
Chapter 4: The Spiral That Led to Rock Bottom	**40**
The Nights That Felt Like Nothing	43
The Mirror That Showed Me Nothing	44
The Conversations I Brushed Off	45
The Inner Collapse	46
The Message That Changed Everything	47
When Amber Walked In	48
Understanding the Spiral	49
Face Your Spiral	50
Questions to Reflect On:	50
Final Thoughts – The Moment Everything Changed	51
Chapter 5: The Climb Back Up	**52**
It's not Just About Stopping—It's About Rebuilding	53
The First Few Weeks of Grief	54
Detoxing Life Means More than Stopping Alcohol	55
My Nervous System Was Fried	57
The Small Wins That Saved Me	57
Not Everyone Wanted Me to Heal	58
Facing Myself Was the Real Work	58
Choosing Myself, Over and Over Again	59
Your Climb Starts Here	60
Questions to Reflect On:	60
Final Thoughts – One Step at a Time	61
Chapter 6: Fully Stepping Into the New Life	**62**
How I Maintain My Peace	62
The Hardest Truth: Some People Only Valued Me When I Was Useful to Them	64
Amber: My Anchor in Transformation	64
The Biggest Lesson: Happiness Was Always There	65
The Grounded Moments That Prove It's Real	66

If I Could Tell My Past Self One Thing	67
Stepping Into Your New Life	68
Questions to Reflect On:	68
Final Thoughts—This Is Just the Start	68

Chapter 7: Manifestation, Reprogramming, and Building a New Reality   70

From Calm to Conscious Creation	70
The Power of Reprogramming Your Mind	71
Rituals That Rewired Me	72
Where Energy Goes, Energy Flows	72
A Human Moment – Life Still Happens	73
The Dream That Changed Everything	74
This is Where Manifestation Gets Real	74
Let Go of the Old Story	74
Your Turn – Reflect, Rewire, Reclaim	75
Final Thoughts – The Door Was Always Open	75

Chapter 8: Rewiring Your Identity and Creating Real Change   77

Letting Go of Who I Thought I Had to Be	78
Micro-Moment: The Day I Stopped Trying to Convince People	78
The Habits That Helped Me Rewire	79
The Rise of Emotional Maturity	80
A Hard Truth: I Used to Be Fickle	80
The "Let Them" Theory Changed Everything	81
The Power of Alignment	81
Mini Crash Moments – But Now I Deal With Them	82
Micro-Moment: Realising I'd Never Put Myself First	82
Who Are You Becoming?	83
Questions to Reflect On:	83
Final Thoughts: Change Is Who You Are Now	84

Chapter 9: Becoming Who I Was Always Meant To Be   85

From Overgiver to Energy Protector	86
Amber: The Light That Never Left	87
The Hard Mirror of Family & Legacy	87

A Moment That Changed Everything	88
Micro-Moments of Becoming	89
From People-Pleasing to Personal Power	89
The New Me Isn't Perfect—But He's Whole	90
Final Thoughts: Becoming is a Choice	91

Chapter 10: Living the Truth, Not Just Speaking It — **93**

When Truth Becomes Your Default	93
The Power of Silence and Alignment	94
From People-Pleasing to Peacekeeping	95
One of the Biggest Emotional Shifts	96
Practical Rituals I Live By Now	96
Questions to Reflect On:	97
Legacy, Impact, and What's Next	97
Final Thoughts: Truth Lived > Truth Spoken	98

Chapter 11: The Journey Continues — **99**

Choosing the Higher Path When It's Hard	99
Supporting Others Without Losing Myself	100
Watching Others Shift Because of Your Growth	101
Seeing Myself Through My Family's Eyes	102
Letting Go of Those Who Only Liked the Old Me	102
I Don't Run From Emotions Any More	103
Final Thoughts: The Journey Is Still Ongoing	103
Questions to Reflect On:	104

Chapter 12: This Is Just the Beginning — **105**

The Truth About Healing	105
Who You Are Now	106
What Comes Next?	107
From Chaos to Clarity—For Good	107
What I Know Now	108
Your Invitation	108
Final Words	109

Chapter 13: Your Turn to Break Free — **111**

This Book Was Never Just About Me	111

Where You Go From Here	112
Start Where You Are	113
You Will Fall. But You'll Rise Faster	114
Your Truth Deserves Space	114
Questions to Reflect On:	114
Final Affirmations: I Am Breaking Free	115
Bonus Section: Letter to My Younger Self	116
Now It's Your Turn	118
Your Clarity Begins Here	118
Affirmations for the Journey	119
Words That Help You Break Free – Recommended Reading	121
Resource Section – For When You Need It Most	122
Acknowledgements	123
About the Author	124
Join the Movement	125

Introduction

Why This Book Exists & Who It's For

The Pain You're Feeling Right Now

If you're reading this, you probably feel stuck. Maybe you don't even know how you got here, but you do know one thing: this isn't the life you wanted.

Perhaps you feel like you're constantly battling a darkness within—a relentless cycle of self-sabotage that keeps pulling you under.

Maybe you've tried to change. You've told yourself this is the last time, the last mistake, the last chance…

But somehow, you always end up back in the same place, making the same choices, feeling the same pain.

You feel like you're trapped in a loop.

You get up every morning, go through the motions, and keep waiting for something—*anything*—to change.

But deep down, you're scared. Scared that this is all there is. Scared that maybe this is just who you are.

I get it. Because I was you.

I know what it's like to wake up feeling exhausted, empty, lost. I know what it's like to hate yourself for your choices but not know how to stop making them. I know what it's like to feel like you've already fucked up so much that you'll never be able to fix it.

And I also know that this feeling of being trapped—this quiet, aching hunger for *something more*—is a deeply human experience.

But I also know this: **It doesn't have to stay this way.**

And if you give me a chance, I'm going to show you exactly how to break free and build a life filled with clarity and purpose.

Why I'm the One Writing This Book

This isn't just another self-help book full of empty inspiration and cliché advice.

I'm not here to give you vague motivational quotes that sound nice but don't actually help.

I'm not going to tell you to *"just think positive"* or *"believe in yourself"* and expect that to change your life.

I'm here because I've lived through these feelings and situations too.

For years, I was trapped in self-destruction. I numbed myself with alcohol, drugs, gambling, toxic cycles, and self-sabotage. I spent my life chasing highs and running from reality because I didn't know how to exist without chaos.

And then, one night, everything crashed down. I hit rock bottom in a way that shattered me. I thought I had nothing left. I thought I had ruined everything.

But in that moment—when I felt like I had completely lost control—I made a choice.

I chose to fight for myself.

I chose to break the cycle.

And I chose to build a life that actually meant something.

And now, I want to help you do the same—by sharing the brutal truth, the practical steps, and the emotional shifts that changed everything for me, and can do the same for you.

What You'll Get from This Book

This book isn't just about my story. It's about *yours*. It's about guiding you through your own transformation. It's about helping you see where you're stuck, why you keep repeating the same patterns, and how you can finally take control.

By the time you finish this book, you'll understand:

- ✓ *Why you've been trapped in cycles of self-sabotage (even if you don't realise it).*

- ✓ *The hard truth about why change is so difficult (and why most people never actually commit to it).*

- ✓ *The exact steps I took to rebuild my life from the ground up.*

✔️ *How to rewire your mind, escape toxic patterns, and create real, lasting transformation.*

This isn't just a book. **It's a roadmap out of hell.** A practical guide to finding your own clarity. And if you're ready—**I'm going to show you the way out.**

Chapter 1: The Breaking Point

I don't know what time it was. I just remember staring at my phone, watching the minutes disappear, feeling like I was outside my own body. A hollow ache had settled deep in my stomach—a physical manifestation of the emptiness that had become my constant companion.

The house was quiet. Too quiet. The kind of quiet that isn't peaceful—it's heavy. Suffocating. A silence that presses against your chest and makes it difficult to breathe. It felt lonely, isolated, almost as if I could hear the pounding of my heart and the relentless spiralling of my thoughts. The energy had been sucked out of the room, leaving everything drained and grey. There was no colour, no life. Just me, existing.

I had been drinking. Again. Another weekend lost to the same cycle—one that felt less like living and more like running. Running from myself. Running from my emotions. Running from the stark reality that, no matter what I did, I was slowly destroying everything good in my life. But this time, something felt fundamentally different.

This wasn't just another hangover. This wasn't just regret. This was heavier. A bone-deep weariness that suggested I might never truly escape this pattern.

I could feel it physically. Anxiety gripped my chest like a vice, a crushing weight pressing down on me. My body felt weak, exhausted, as though every cell was screaming for respite. My hands were cold and clammy, trembling under the weight of guilt, shame, and fear. The reality of my self-destruction was finally staring me in the face—it was undeniable. Unavoidable.

I felt sick—physically, mentally, emotionally. And for the first time, I truly didn't know if I could take this any more. My mind echoed with the thoughts: You're a failure. You'll never be good enough.

It wasn't that I wanted to die. But I also didn't know how to keep living like this. If there had been a button in front of me that said, "Stop Draining Emotions", I would've pressed it. Without hesitation. Without thought.

My mind circled relentlessly: I've let everyone down. I'm failing. I'm trapped. And deep down, the hardest truth hit me—I wasn't just letting others down, I was letting myself down.

How could I show up for anyone else when I wasn't even showing up for myself?

One thing I've learned since then is that you must treat yourself with the same compassion, love, and respect you give to others. Many of us never extend that same kindness to ourselves. We don't prioritise our own peace or self-worth—yet that's exactly what we need most. Little did I know, learning to give that kindness to myself would be the key to unlocking the prison I had built.

My phone sat heavy in my hand. I kept checking it, rereading the same messages I'd sent, hoping somehow the words or the reality would change. Maybe I was overreacting. Maybe the next day would be better.

But deep down, I knew the truth. Tomorrow wasn't going to be fine.

This was the moment everything crashed down.

Without even thinking, I texted my mum.

"Mam, can you come over?"

The response was immediate, like she'd been waiting for this very message for years.

"On my way, son."

She knew. They all knew—Amber, my mum, my dad, my sister. They had all been watching me spiral. Witnessing the patterns. Waiting for the moment when everything had to come crashing down. Because you can't keep repeating the same behaviours and expect a different outcome.

The sound of her knock was like a gunshot, shattering the oppressive silence.

Forcing myself to the door felt impossible—like pushing against concrete. But as soon as she stepped inside and her eyes met mine, I broke completely.

I wasn't just crying—I was falling apart. Exhausted. Empty. Numb.

She wrapped her arms around me, and I sank into her, gripping on like she was the only thing stopping me from disappearing completely.

"I know, son," she whispered, her voice breaking.

She'd always been there—my mum. Alongside my dad and sister. Always picking up the pieces. Always holding me up when I couldn't hold myself.

They never gave up on me—even when giving up would have been easier.

"I can't do this any more", I managed to say between my sobs. And this time, I truly meant it. This wasn't just guilt. This wasn't just a comedown or a crash. This was rock bottom.

Amber was on the train home when I messaged her. "Do you mind getting a taxi? I'm not feeling great."

She replied quickly, her instincts immediately sensing something was wrong. "What's happened?"

I paused, then answered. "Mam's here. Don't worry. Everything's come to a head. I'll talk when you're back."

Of course, she called. She always showed up. Emotionally present, aware, strong—even when it broke her heart to see me trapped in this cycle.

Her loyalty was unshakeable. Her love, unconditional. Even when I didn't deserve it.

"I'm just glad your mum's there", she said softly. Her voice was steady but laced with emotion. "I didn't want you to be alone."

When she walked through the door, I saw it in her face—relief, worry, heartbreak. She'd carried the weight of this for years, waiting for it to explode. And now it had.

She came over, wrapped her arms around me, and whispered, "I'm here for you."

And I let go. I leaned into her because I had nothing left.

That moment, something inside me shattered—but not in a way that broke me further. Something cracked open. Something honest. Something real. This was the crossroads.

My life. My relationships. My health. My future. My sanity. My self-respect—everything was at stake.

And my greatest fear? Losing Amber. Losing myself. Losing it all.

Amber looked into my eyes. Calm. Direct. Strong.

"Something has to give", she said quietly. Like she could see directly into my soul.

She was right. I couldn't keep numbing myself. Couldn't keep running. Couldn't keep drowning.

I'd spent years in this cycle. Choosing short-term relief over long-term peace. Choosing chaos over clarity. Choosing destruction over healing. Choosing to stay stuck because I was too scared of what might happen if I changed.

But now? Now, change wasn't optional. It was survival.

Tony Robbins says, "Change happens when the pain of staying the same is greater than the pain of change."

I understood that now. Deeply.

I'd always known I was meant for more. I had so much to give. So much to offer. Outside of the chaos, I was kind, loving, supportive, compassionate.

Yet here I was — drowning in a cycle I had created.

And as Amber held me and my mum sat quietly nearby, I finally made the decision — I was going to break free.

Because at rock bottom, the only way left… is up. And for the first time in years, I chose to rise.

But how? That was the question echoing through the silence.

Chapter 2: Echoes of Early Years – Unpacking Your Foundations

During the week, our home had a rhythm. We had routines, dinner times, telly on in the background—a sort of steady hum that made things feel normal. But when the weekend came around, everything picked up pace.

The volume went up. The energy shifted. Music filled the house, people came and went, and the vibe became lively—full of laughter, conversation, and that weekend buzz. As a kid, I didn't fully understand it, but I felt it. There was an intensity to it that sometimes left me overstimulated or struggling to wind down, especially when I was tired.

I remember lying in bed some nights, hoping the noise would settle. Not because I wasn't welcome or loved—I absolutely was—but because I didn't have the tools back then to explain that I needed a bit of calm. I didn't know how to say, "It's just a bit too much for me."

Now, looking back, I can see it clearly: my parents were letting off steam after a long, hard week. It was their way of enjoying themselves. There was no bad intent—just different needs under one roof. And as a sensitive kid, I sometimes found that tough to navigate.

Questions to Reflect On:

Were there moments in childhood where your environment felt fast-paced or intense, even if it was filled with love?

Did you ever wish for quiet or space without knowing how to ask for it?

What did emotional safety look like to you growing up?

Insight

Sometimes it's not about what was done wrong—it's about what wasn't yet understood. A child might not know how to articulate their needs, and parents might not see what isn't being said. But even without blame, those early dynamics shape how we learn to self-regulate, communicate, and seek connection.

Trying to Belong

At some point, I started leaning into the weekend energy. Instead of pulling away from it, I tried to be part of it. I figured if I joined in—laughed along, danced, sang—maybe I'd feel more connected.

I remember the first time someone praised me for singing. That moment lit something up in me. I felt seen. Recognised. Like I mattered. That feeling stuck with me. And for a long time after, I chased it.

Performing became my bridge. If I could make people laugh or entertain them, I felt like I belonged. Like I had something to offer. That I wasn't just there—I was part of the moment.

Questions to Reflect On:

How did you seek connection when you were young?

Was there a moment when you realised that entertaining others got you attention?

Are there parts of yourself you still feel you have to "prove" today?

Insight

When you're young, connection is everything. If performance becomes the way to connect, it becomes easy to tie your worth to how others respond to you—rather than how you feel about yourself. It's not attention we crave. It's acceptance.

Becoming the Showman

That's how "The Showman" was born—the part of me that showed up, smiled, made people laugh, and kept the mood light. I became skilled at reading rooms and adapting to what people needed. It didn't feel like effort at the time—it felt like instinct.

But underneath it all, I was still learning who I was. Was I naturally funny, or did I just learn it got me noticed? Was I confident, or just good at covering nerves with a joke?

That's the thing about childhood roles—we grow into them, and sometimes we forget we ever had a choice.

Questions to Reflect On:

What role did you play in your family or social group growing up?

Did it feel natural, or did it feel like something you had to be?

Is that role still showing up in your adult life—and is it helping or hindering you?

Insight

We often form identities that helped us get through childhood—but those identities aren't always aligned with who we truly are. Healing is about meeting the version of yourself that existed before the performance.

Living Between Two Worlds

My early years weren't extreme. There was no dramatic trauma. I was loved, cared for, supported. But there was also inconsistency—moments that felt emotionally overwhelming or difficult to read. And as someone who felt things deeply, I picked up on all of it.

One moment, things were calm and close. The next, the mood might change. A shift in energy, a raised voice, a loud night. It wasn't bad—just unpredictable. And for someone like me, that unpredictability wired me to be on alert. To adapt. To adjust before anything even happened.

That's how I learned to shape-shift. Not in a manipulative way—just in a way that kept me safe. Or at least, made me feel safe.

Questions to Reflect On:

Have you ever felt like you had to adapt quickly depending on the mood or energy around you?

Are you someone who picks up on tension before it's spoken?

Do you feel exhausted by constantly trying to "read the room"?

Insight

Being emotionally in tune is a gift. But when it stems from a need to stay safe or keep the peace, it can become exhausting. Recognising that pattern is the first step to choosing presence over performance.

Growing Up Sensitive

I've always felt things more than most people around me. As a kid, I noticed details others missed—tone shifts, energy changes, what people meant even when they didn't say it.

Sometimes that made me feel like I was "too much". Too emotional. Too intense. So I turned it down. I learned how to fit in instead of stand out. But every time I did, I moved a little further from myself.

And that's a quiet kind of loneliness—the kind where you're surrounded by people, but unsure if anyone really sees the authentic you.

Questions to Reflect On:

Were you ever told you were "too sensitive"?

What did you start hiding to be accepted?

How much of you today is shaped by what others expected?

Insight

Sensitivity isn't a flaw, it's a gift that needs care and validation. Learning to honour it rather than edit it is a huge part of coming home to yourself.

Looking Back with Clarity and Compassion

Now, as an adult, I can hold both truths at once: that I was deeply loved, and that I still had moments of emotional confusion. That my parents did everything they could, and that I still sometimes struggled to find my place within it all.

There's no blame in that. Just understanding. I can look back now and see the context, not just the feeling. I know everyone was doing their best—and I genuinely believe that. But as a child, without the language to explain what I needed, I internalised things that shaped how I saw myself and the world.

And this chapter? It's not about calling anyone out. It's about calling my patterns out—the ones I carried long after I left that house. The ones that shaped relationships, self-worth, and how I handled discomfort.

Because once I understood the roots, I could start changing the growth.

Final Questions to Reflect On:

What parts of your childhood feel complicated—and can you see them with compassion instead of judgement?

Have you ever felt like you had to choose between being yourself and being accepted?

What would it feel like to stop performing and simply be?

———

Insight

You were never too much. You were never too needy. You were never asking for too much by needing space, calm, or connection.

You were simply feeling. Learning. Responding.

And now, you're rewriting the story.

———

Final Insight

This chapter isn't about blame. It's about awareness. When you become aware of the foundations that shaped you, you reclaim the power to rebuild. You don't have to keep living the same story on repeat. You don't have to keep wearing masks just to feel safe or seen. Your story isn't over. It's just beginning.

And here's the truth: You're not too broken. You're not too far gone. You're not unworthy of healing. You were shaped by your survival.

But now? You get to choose your growth.

This is your turning point.

From chaos… to clarity.

Chapter 3: Slipping Into the Cycle

I never planned for it to become a cycle. Nobody does.

It's like stepping onto a carousel—the music's bright, the lights are flashing, and it feels like harmless fun. You enjoy the ride, maybe a little too much, and then suddenly you realise it's not stopping. You're just going round and round, faster and faster, and the initial thrill has morphed into a dizzying, sickening loop.

At first, it wasn't self-destruction—it was just fun. That's the insidious lie it always tells you.

The house parties. The music shaking the walls, bass that vibrates through your bones. Laughter echoing through the rooms, fuelled by whatever was going—lager, vodka, gin, whisky. We drank it all.

There was a buzz in knowing I could walk into a room and become the heartbeat of it. For a few hours, I belonged. No overthinking awkward silences, no anxiety about not fitting in, no suffocating emptiness. Just the raw, unfiltered energy of the moment.

I felt alive when people were having a good time, when they were engaged, interested, connected. That's what made me feel like I mattered. And I loved to sing—always have. Loved to dance too. So I'd become the life and soul of the party: funny, energetic, lost in the music.

We had some great times. Genuinely fun moments. I can't deny it, and I can't say I didn't enjoy it—at the time.

It's just that eventually, the cycle took over. It twisted that fun into something darker. Something that quietly, insidiously, started to own me.

The house would start off mellow—just a few mates chatting, the music low—but it never stayed like that. It always escalated. The volume went up, more people showed up, and suddenly, it was a full-blown party.

For a while, that's all it was. Just a few drinks to take the edge off. Just the weekend—a chance to blow off steam after a long week. Just chasing the high of music, laughter, connection.

Just… just.

That word hides so much. Because what begins as "just now and then" becomes "just this weekend," then "just to cope", until eventually, it's just who you are. It's no longer a break from reality—it becomes your reality.

I never made a conscious decision to spiral. The descent was subtle. A slow unravelling disguised as fun. Until the highs weren't optional—they were necessary. A lifeline. A way to drown out everything I didn't want to face.

The Early Signs—Feeling the Pull

The weekends had a rhythm of their own.

During the week, I grafted. I've always worked hard, always wanted more—building businesses, chasing progress, trying to build a future.

From Monday to Friday, life looked fine from the outside. But when the weekend hit, the switch flipped. I'd become the Showman again. Nicky, the entertainer. The funny one. The one who brought the buzz.

I'd tell jokes, project energy, and feed off the vibe in the room. If the energy dropped, I'd lift it. I wanted to leave people better than I found them.

And it felt good—knowing I was making people laugh and enjoy themselves.

But it also disconnected me from myself. I gave too much away. Overwhelmed myself. Depleted my own energy trying to manage the energy of the room. It was people-pleasing dressed up as fun.

As the saying goes, people-pleasing is self-betrayal with good branding. But you don't need to be liked. You need to be respected. And respect comes from boundaries—not bending.

I played the role perfectly. But what people didn't see was what came after.

The crash. The regret. The heavy weight in my chest. The hours lying in bed panicking, replaying conversations, wondering what I'd said or if I'd upset Amber. Scrolling through my phone, rereading messages, trying to piece together the night like a puzzle that never quite fit.

I'd lie there, feeling like I was in the wrong body. Exhausted. Anxious. Full of guilt and shame. Running from myself. Only now I was sprinting.

Sometimes, the crash came mid-party — while everyone else was still laughing, still up. That's when the mask would start to slip. The novelty would wear off. My mind would catch up with my body, and I'd realise: this isn't who I want to be.

The Showman would fade. And anxiety would flood in.

Palpitations. Shaky hands. Shallow breaths. I'd lie down, trying to breathe through it, convinced I was about to have a panic attack — or worse. And yet, I'd still go again the next weekend.

Because the cycle had already taken hold.

―――

The Cycle Tightens Its Grip

What started as a way to let off steam soon became my identity. The weekends weren't about enjoyment any more. They were about escape.

I didn't drink because I loved alcohol. I drank because it connected me to chaos. It gave me a way to run. To avoid my thoughts. To silence the stillness. To dodge the discomfort I didn't want to face. Especially during my teenage years.

While my mates were out making genuine connections, going to new places, I was stuck in house party loops. Isolated in a different way. Missing out on experiences that shaped others.

And when you're living like that, your body doesn't get a break. You spend Monday to Wednesday trying to recover. By Thursday, you start to feel normal again. Then Friday comes... and you start it all over again.

———

Questions to Reflect On:

- Do you notice patterns in your life that repeat—even when they hurt you?
- Are you waiting to "feel normal again", only to start the cycle all over?

———

Insight

Many of us don't realise how much these cycles deprive us of real happiness until we've missed out on everything that truly matters. The danger isn't in one bad night—it's in how easily one night becomes a lifestyle. A lifestyle that steals your time, your energy, your future.

———

The Emotional Aftermath — The Shame Spiral

The come-down wasn't just physical, it was emotional carnage.

I'd feel manic. Anxious. Guilt-ridden. Like I'd ruined everything. Like I'd let everyone down — especially myself.

I'd isolate. Try to act normal. Smile through it. But inside, I was empty.

I'd tell myself stories to justify it:

"Everyone does this."

"I need a release."

"It was just one weekend."

"I work hard during the week — I deserve it."

But deep down, I knew the truth. I wasn't chasing fun. I was chasing connection. Chasing novelty. Running from stillness. Because stillness made me feel everything I was trying to avoid.

And ADHD made it worse. Before I was diagnosed, I didn't understand why the crashes hit me harder. But now I know — ADHD brains struggle with dopamine regulation.

When you add alcohol or drugs into the mix, it messes with your neurochemistry. The highs hit harder. But the crash? It hits harder too. You don't just feel tired. Your brain dips below baseline. Foggy. Flat. Low.

―――――

Fact Check: ADHD and dopamine imbalance are real. Studies show that people with ADHD often have lower baseline dopamine. After a high, they don't just feel low—they crash. That explained a lot of what I went through.

―――――

The Moment the Mask Slipped

I was deep in the cycle. The parties were regular. I'd be the life of the room—until I wasn't. There'd come a point in the night when my body would just reject it all. My nervous system would shut down. The anxiety would take over.

I'd feel like I was going to have a heart attack. I'd have to lie down, heart racing, trying to catch my breath, spinning out.

And I'd still do it again the next weekend. Because that's what the cycle does—it convinces you to forget. It tells you next time will be different. That you'll stop at one. That it won't hit you as hard.

But it always does.

―――――

The Inner Conflict—Knowing but Ignoring

There were signs. Conversations with Amber. Quiet talks with my mum and dad.

"We can't keep doing this."

"You're going to lose something."

"We're worried."

I knew they were right. But I didn't stop.

I told myself I was still young. That because I grafted through the week, I was allowed to blow off steam. It was just what people around here do.

But that's the illusion.

Even in the heart of the chaos, there was always a whisper. That small voice saying, "This isn't you. You're better than this."

But I'd drown it out. Another drink. Another night. Another laugh. Not ready to face the discomfort of that truth.

But the whisper persisted. It always does.

You keep ignoring that voice, and suddenly, you're 30, 40, 50—and nothing's changed. Because if your foundation is chaos, it doesn't matter what you build. It will crumble eventually.

I lost so much time. My teens. My early twenties. Weekends I'll never get back. Time I could've spent growing, learning, connecting. Instead, I was stuck in a loop of hangovers and missed chances. Chasing moments that didn't matter while ignoring the ones that did.

Questions to Reflect On:

- What illusions are keeping you stuck right now?
- What are you convincing yourself is "fine", even when it's not?
- Are you living the life you want—or just the one you're used to?

Insight

Cycles become familiar. Comfortable, even. But just because something feels normal doesn't mean it's right. The truth often feels uncomfortable—but it's that discomfort that leads to growth. You can't heal in the same environment that broke you.

The Role of Others—Enablers and Eye-Openers

Some people enabled me. Some were friends. Some were family. Others were just drinking mates I thought were friends—until they disappeared when I hit rock bottom.

But the ones who stayed? They mattered.

Amber never walked away. She didn't shout. She didn't blame. She didn't give ultimatums. She sat with me in the mess. Calm. Compassionate. Real. We had quiet, honest conversations.

She showed me that connection doesn't come from chaos—it comes from clarity. From truth. From accountability.

She loved me enough to believe I could change—even when I didn't believe it myself.

The Breaking Point (Before the Breakdown)

There wasn't just one big "aha" moment, there were hundreds of small ones. Whispers. Nudges. Gut feelings. The messages I'd ignore. The moments I'd dismiss. The pain I'd numb. Until eventually, I couldn't ignore it any more.

I couldn't pretend it was just a phase.

I was tired. Tired of repeating myself. Tired of waking up ashamed. Tired of running from who I really was. The pain of staying the same had finally become greater than the pain of change.

That was the turning point. Not because someone told me to change. But because I finally wanted to.

I was done performing. Done spiralling. Done surviving. I wanted to live.

Final Thoughts—Standing at the Edge

Sometimes, we lose ourselves so deeply in the cycle, we forget who we were before it. But there's always a whisper. There's always a moment. This chapter wasn't just a phase. It was the unravelling.

But unravelling is necessary—because only when everything falls apart can you rebuild with intention.

Your Turn—Reflect, Write, Reclaim

Take a deep breath.

You've just walked through some heavy truth. Now it's time to sit with your own.

Journal prompts:

- What cycles are keeping you stuck right now?
- What do you use to escape? What are you avoiding?
- What does your crash feel like—and what's it trying to tell you?

- Who in your life enables your patterns? Who truly supports your healing?
- What illusion are you living in—and what would it mean to finally break it?

Insight

You can't outrun the crash. But you can choose to rise from it.

This isn't the end of your story—it's the beginning of your freedom.

Chapter 4: The Spiral That Led to Rock Bottom

The walls weren't hiding secrets—they were tired of hearing them. Same patterns. Same promises. Same chaos, just wearing a different mask. The same patterns. The same promises. The same cycles of chaos dressed up as connection.

I'd come home drained and burnt out from work, already feeling tired, and tell myself I was just going out for a pint—my way to shut my mind down and switch off, or so I thought. That one pint before tea would often turn into forgetting to eat altogether, carrying on drinking into the night, leaving me heavy, exhausted, and setting me back yet again.

My mind craved that temporary release from the constant thoughts, the stress, the need to escape and run away, to numb the pain. It wasn't living; it was just existing.

I'd head to the local pub. The background music and chatter were a deceptive comfort, the noise almost making me feel like I wasn't doing anything wrong.

"One won't hurt", I'd tell myself. "I'm entitled to it. I deserve it. I've worked hard."

But that was the lie. It was never just about relaxing and enjoying one drink. My mind, deep down, probably knew it was leading me—or the cycle was taking me—to drown out as much as I could. The dread, fear, and anxiety would be crushing—an out-of-body experience where my soul felt like it wanted to leave. My mind wanted to shut down, and my body yearned to run away.

In those moments, I would hate myself and think the most negative thoughts—the kind I wouldn't wish on my worst enemy. It was heart-wrenching.

It was never about going out. Not for me.

The destruction didn't happen in bars or clubs—it happened in living rooms, kitchens, home bars, wherever we gathered and pretended we were living.

It didn't matter where. The energy was always the same. Familiar. Predictable. Heavy.

At first, it was fun. I won't lie.

There were nights when the laughter was real, when the buzz in the room felt electric, when it seemed like nothing else mattered—and that was the best feeling in the world. The music loud. The conversations deep (or at least, they felt deep at the time). The illusion of freedom stretching late into the night.

One of the most appealing aspects of those early "fun" nights was the feeling of connection, of belonging, of finally letting go and disappearing for a while.

That kept me wanting to go back.

But I lost myself in the cycle. It was an illusion of genuine self. Some parts were genuine—the words to people, the laughter, some connections—but much of it was surface level, fake, unmeaningful. Nothing that would last or was healthy.

It was running, and it was killing me in every way possible.

I was becoming less and less of myself each time, the dissociation and depersonalisation cutting deeper and deeper.

The person I saw in the mirror wasn't the real me. The real me was suppressed, caged up, surrounded by chaos—and shrinking.

Why do we do this to ourselves? Everyone is so different and unique, so why do we care what other people think?

We're never going to be liked or loved by everyone, and we don't need to be. We need to love and respect ourselves first.

But fun has an expiry date. And I passed mine long before I realised it. What started as letting off steam slowly morphed into something darker—something I didn't want to name.

It stopped being about fun. It stopped being about anything. It just became… routine. An unspoken agreement that this was what weekends looked like now.

Drink. Escape. Crash. Regret. Repeat.

And I convinced myself that everyone was the same. I looked around the room and thought we were all spiralling together. But the truth? Not everyone was falling like I was. Some people could pick themselves up and carry on like nothing happened.

But I couldn't.

I wasn't just tired after a night like that—I was shattered. Emotionally. Mentally. Physically.

I hit the lowest point when the emotion got too much and my body and mind took over—putting me in survival mode to the point where I couldn't leave my bed for days. I isolated myself, watching programmes I liked just to numb the pain. My emotions were switched off, almost as if a button had been pressed.

After that, I was dissociated—not present (not that I was present much anyway), completely numb to emotion. I remember wanting to cry but couldn't bring myself to because I was living in survival mode, filled to the brim with cortisol. I was losing parts of myself in every hangover and didn't even realise how deep I'd sunk.

———

The Nights That Felt Like Nothing

It got to a point where I could predict the script:

- Start drinking. Feel good.
- Get into it. The energy's high.
- Tell myself it's fine. "Just tonight."

- A few more. Lose track of time.
- End the night half-remembering, half-hoping I didn't say something stupid.
- Wake up with guilt sitting in my chest like a brick.
- Swear I'll do better next time.
- Do it again anyway.

I wasn't drinking to socialise. I was drinking to disappear. And in the environment I was in—it didn't raise eyebrows. Because it was normal. Everyone was doing the same. No one was pulling me aside. No one was calling it what it was.

That's the dangerous thing about chaos when it's packaged as routine—it hides in plain sight.

I was in the spiral.

But back then, I didn't know that spiral had an end point. That it would lead me to a moment when everything—my health, my future, my relationships—would hang in the balance.

―――

The Mirror That Showed Me Nothing

There's something eerie about staring into your own eyes and feeling like a stranger.

I remember looking at myself—and also looking back at old photos—and I looked older than I do now. Like a ghost. Fading away. No life in my eyes. Gaunt. Unhappy. Broken.

Sometimes we don't even realise we're not the same person looking back.

I was physically shrinking. My body was begging me to stop. But I didn't care. Not because I didn't want to—but because I wasn't present.

I was checked out. Disconnected from my body. Disconnected from reality. There in the room—but not really there.

I'd speak, laugh, move—but internally, I was in survival mode. Just existing.

When I look back at pictures from that time—it's like looking at a ghost. But I didn't see it then. I was too deep in the spiral to even notice I was fading.

The Conversations I Brushed Off

People tried to reach me. Amber. My mum. My sister. My dad. They weren't shouting. They weren't telling me to stop. But the concern was in their voices, their eyes, their silences.

"Are you alright?"

"You've been tired a lot lately."

"Maybe just have a quiet one this weekend?"

I'd shrug it off. Laugh it off. Downplay it.

"I'm fine."

"I'm just tired."

"I'll take it easy."

Lies. Lies I told to keep them comfortable. Lies I told to avoid looking at what was really going on. Because deep down, I knew they were right.

But I wasn't ready to admit it. Not to them—and certainly not to myself.

———

The Inner Collapse

It wasn't one dramatic moment. It wasn't like a film where everything comes crashing down in one explosive event.

It was slow. Quiet. Chipping away at me, piece by piece.

Until one night… I stopped. I sat in silence. Phone in my hand. Not scrolling. Just staring at it.

I felt detached from my own body. My nervous system was fried. My brain felt foggy. My chest was tight. I wasn't even anxious any more—I was beyond that. I was numb.

That was the moment I realised I wasn't just tired—I was breaking.

I'd hit the point where feeling nothing was no longer an option. Where the numbness couldn't hold back the wave of everything I'd been avoiding. The emotions I'd buried were breaking through—and I couldn't ignore them any longer.

And then it hit me: This wasn't about being tired. I was done. Done pretending. Done performing. Done lying. Done escaping.

I was spiralling toward rock bottom—and the bottom was coming fast.

The Message That Changed Everything

I know I mentioned this earlier, but it's worth repeating—because this was the moment everything truly changed.

I texted my mum. I didn't even know what to write. I think I just said: 'Can you come over?'

She didn't ask questions. Didn't hesitate."

"On my way, son."

I'll never forget the sound of her knock. It hit me like a bullet. When she stepped through the door and saw me—I couldn't hold it in any more. I collapsed into her arms.

I couldn't hold it in — I was done. Exhausted. Broken.

That moment of collapsing into her arms was pivotal. I needed to be held because I couldn't hold myself. I felt weak, breathless, almost like my body wanted to give up and leave me. I even thought it might be easier to let it. But then that fighter instinct kicked in. We all need to be fighters.

That was the moment everything changed. I needed my mother there to hold me, and for me to have the realisation that this was it—all or nothing.

When Amber Walked In

Later that night, Amber came home. She walked in, saw me with my mum, and I saw two things flash in her eyes: relief and pain.

The unspoken message in her eyes was clear: relief that it had finally come to a head because it was inevitable, and maybe this would be the point of change, but also deep pain at seeing me put myself through so much. She always knew it cut me just as deep as the people I was hurting.

She was strong. Always had been. Strong even when she shouldn't have had to be. She'd carried the emotional weight of my choices with grace—never turning her back on me.

But she looked done. Not in a way that said "I'm leaving", but in a way that said, "You can't keep doing this to yourself. To us."

She wrapped her arms around me and said it quietly: "Something has to give."

And I nodded. Because I knew. I had two choices:

➡ Keep going and lose everything.

➡ Face it, and finally fight for myself.

For the first time in years, I chose me. This was the catalyst for that internal shift—the rock bottom moment described in Chapter 1, the culmination of this spiral.

―――

Understanding the Spiral

Let's break it down.

These spirals don't just happen. They're built over time—layer by layer. Fun becomes routine. Routine becomes addiction. Addiction becomes identity.

For me, the spiral looked like:

- Living for weekends.
- Chasing the high.
- Losing days to recovery.
- Feeling shame and guilt.
- Promising to stop.
- Repeating it all again.

It wasn't about alcohol. It wasn't even about chaos. It was about disconnection. From myself. From my purpose. From the truth.

And when you live disconnected for long enough, you forget what wholeness even feels like.

Face Your Spiral

Questions to Reflect On:

Grab your journal or notepad. This is your moment to go deeper:

- What does your "spiral" look like right now?
- What are you using to numb yourself—and what are you avoiding?
- Who has quietly tried to help you? Have you listened?
- What lies have you been telling yourself to justify your choices?
- What would it mean for you to say, "Something has to give"—and mean it?

Insight

The truth doesn't hurt nearly as much as living a lie.

When you stop performing and start being, healing can begin.

Final Thoughts – The Moment Everything Changed

This chapter wasn't rock bottom. But it was the last step before the fall. It was the moment of truth. The quiet reckoning. The one you don't see coming until it's already here.

I was lucky. I had people who saw me. Held me. Sat with me when I couldn't sit with myself. But not everyone gets that chance.

So if you're here—reading this—this is your moment. Not a breakdown. A breakthrough.

You don't have to hit rock bottom to wake up. You can stop now. Right here. And if you've already fallen? You can rise.

Because your story isn't over. It's just beginning.

Chapter 5: The Climb Back Up

There was no miracle moment. No bright light. No cinematic turning point where everything suddenly clicked and I felt healed. There was just this quiet, heavy silence—and the decision to not go back.

That was it.

The climb back up didn't start with fireworks. It started with stillness. The kind of stillness I had spent years running from.

After the chaos had subsided, the silence felt like a rollercoaster. At times, it was peaceful—a welcome break from the storm. But other times, it became deafening. It allowed the voices in my head to get louder, to question me, to try and pull me back into the old ways. I'd later understand these weren't truths—they were just ingrained cycles, patterns, and false beliefs begging to be broken.

And that's where the real battle began.

The climb back up isn't some one-size-fits-all solution. It's a deep, confronting process. You have to look within—really look. You've got to get honest about how you got here. You need to face the ways you've kept yourself stuck, the things you've been using to numb yourself, bring to light the parts of yourself you've ignored or hidden. Because it's not about dragging more things into your life. It's about remembering what was already there. Knowing that you are enough.

You are enough.

That's the truth you have to come back to over and over again.

I started asking myself three simple questions every time the urge to spiral came knocking:

- "Is this going to set me back?"
- "Am I running away?"
- "Am I feeling this, or avoiding it?"

That became my check-in. Was it hard? Brutally. But not doing it would've been harder in the long run.

"If you don't sacrifice for what you want, what you want becomes the sacrifice."

It's not Just About Stopping—It's About Rebuilding

I thought if I just stopped drinking, everything would magically get better. I thought the fog would lift and I'd feel alive again.

But sobriety didn't give me clarity. It gave me truth.

And the truth? The truth was brutal. I realised how far I'd drifted from myself. I wasn't connected to my body, my heart, or the moment in front of me. I wasn't living—I was just existing.

Alcohol wasn't the root. It was a symptom. A mask. A mute button I pressed to quiet the noise. When I took it away, that noise came back full volume.

And what did I hear the loudest? The fear of my own potential.

I always knew deep down I was meant for more. That I could help people. That I could love deeply and live fully and make a real difference. But I'd buried that truth under chaos. And now, with nothing to numb it, I had to face it.

The trauma. The guilt. The boredom. The lost years. The version of me I no longer recognised.

It was like taking the lid off a boiling pot. Everything came spilling out.

―――

The First Few Weeks of Grief

The first few weeks were both tough and eye-opening. Grieving the chaos, the routine, the buzz, the false identity of being "the fun one." And then there were the weekends, the dopamine hits, the people I thought were friends. The version of me I'd built just to survive.

Grief doesn't only happen when someone dies. It happens when you die—when an old version of you fades and a new one starts to emerge.

I was raw, like my skin had been peeled back. Irritable. Restless. Emotional. Exposed.

The questions came flooding in:

Who am I without the parties?

Who am I when I'm not the loudest person in the room?

Who am I when I'm just... quiet?

Who am I?

The quiet was terrifying—because it made me feel everything I'd been avoiding. But somewhere in that space, buried beneath the shame and fear... there was something else.

Hope.

Detoxing Life Means More than Stopping Alcohol

For me, detoxing wasn't just about ditching the drink, it was about unlearning everything that enabled the spiral.

For you, it might not be alcohol, it might be:

- Numbing with substances.
- Overworking to avoid emotions.
- Scrolling to run from the silence.

- 💔 Staying in toxic relationships because chaos feels familiar.
- Eating to soothe, starving to control.
- Sleeping all day or not at all.
- People-pleasing until *you* disappear.
- Performing just to be accepted.
- Creating drama because peace feels too unfamiliar.

These are the coping strategies that seem harmless, even normal—but they're not. They're symptoms. And once I stopped drinking, I had to face them too.

I had to set boundaries. With people, yes—but more importantly, with myself.

I had to stop entertaining anything or anyone that only loved the broken version of me. Because healing makes people uncomfortable. And not everyone will come with you.

That meant saying no. That meant walking away. That meant hearing the silence in friendships that only thrived on chaos—and choosing to sit in that silence instead of filling it with noise.

I had to learn to be with myself—no phone, no distraction, no numbing. And that was terrifying at first.

But slowly—quietly—I started to hear myself again.

My Nervous System Was Fried

No one talks about this enough. When you've been living in chaos, your nervous system doesn't just reset. Even when you're doing all the right things—sleeping, eating, moving—you still feel wired, anxious, like your body doesn't know how to be calm.

Busy places overwhelmed me. My breathing was shallow. My muscles were tight. Even silence felt loud.

That's trauma. That's what it looks like when your system's been running on adrenaline and cortisol for years.

Healing isn't just emotional, it's physical and neurological, and it takes time. So. Much. Time.

The Small Wins That Saved Me

I had to stop thinking big. I couldn't plan five years ahead. I just had to get through today.

- ✅ Get out of bed
- ✅ Drink water
- ✅ Move
- ✅ Eat
- ✅ Breathe
- ✅ Don't escape

That was my recovery plan. Not dramatic. Not impressive. But real. Each choice was a brick. Each day, a small rebuild. Each moment I didn't spiral was a win.

I'd ask myself: "Am I running away?" "Is this my truth, or a false belief?"

That was enough.

Not Everyone Wanted Me to Heal

When you change, you become a mirror. Some people aren't ready to see themselves—so they project it back onto you.

You stop drinking, and they say you're boring.

You set a boundary, and they say you've changed.

You speak truth, and they call you intense.

But that's not about you. That's their discomfort with your growth. Let them be uncomfortable. The people who matter won't leave. They'll lean in.

Facing Myself Was the Real Work

This was the hardest part—taking accountability for what I'd done. For the damage. For the trust I had broken. For the people I'd hurt—especially Amber.

She never gave up on me. But that didn't mean she wasn't wounded.

I had to earn it back. Not with words. Not with promises. But with presence. Show up. Stay consistent. Be who I said I was. That's how you rebuild trust.

And most importantly—I had to rebuild it with myself.

Choosing Myself, Over and Over Again

The urges didn't vanish. The temptation didn't disappear. But I got better at listening to what I really needed underneath it.

Sometimes it was taking time to rest. Sometimes it was finding connection. Sometimes it was just sitting with the discomfort and breathing through it.

The truth is:

📌 One more time is never just one more time.

📌 Escaping is a short-term fix with long-term damage.

📌 Peace isn't found in noise—it's found in presence.

And I was finally starting to feel it.

One day, driving back from my vocal coach, music playing, singing at the top of my lungs—I felt peace.

Not hype. Not chaos. Just presence. I felt alive again. Not all at once. Not every day. But in moments, in conversations, in early mornings, in silence.

That's what I was climbing toward.

———

"The best time to plant a tree was 20 years ago. The second-best time is now." — Chinese Proverb

———

Your Climb Starts Here

Questions to Reflect On:

- What parts of your life feel like they're built on chaos?
- What are you scared will happen if you stop escaping?
- Who do you become when you're no longer running?
- What "small wins" can you commit to today?
- Who or what do you need to detox from your life right now?

———

Insight

Recovery doesn't start with a grand plan, it starts with a choice. A single, honest decision to stop abandoning yourself—and to come back home.

Final Thoughts – One Step at a Time

The climb isn't glamorous. It's messy. Emotional. Tiring. But it's real.

And if you're in it right now—if you're sitting in the rubble of your old life wondering whether you can rebuild—let this be your sign:

You can. Not by being perfect. But by being present.

You don't have to do it all today. You just have to start.

This isn't the end of your story. It's the beginning of your return. Back to who you were always meant to be.

Chapter 6: Fully Stepping Into the New Life

The contrast between my life now and the life I once lived is like night and day. For years, I was stuck in a cycle of self-destruction—chasing highs, numbing pain, running from reality. I convinced myself that chaos was normal, that the crash after the buzz was just part of life.

But now? Everything is different.

That quiet, heavy silence I experienced at the start of my recovery—the one that used to feel so unsettling—has transformed. Now, silence is a sanctuary. It's where I reconnect with myself, not where I run from myself.

I wake up feeling calm, connected, and most importantly, content. Not every day is perfect—but every day is mine. I live with intention. I protect my peace. I no longer chase external highs because I've found something deeper: fulfilment.

This chapter isn't just about what changed for me. It's about showing you what's possible for you too. Because breaking free was just the beginning. Staying free? That's the real work.

How I Maintain My Peace

Peace isn't passive. It's not something you stumble into or earn when the world finally stops demanding so much from you. It's a commitment. A conscious decision you make every single day.

For me, that means:

✓ Enforcing boundaries – If something or someone doesn't align with my healing, I walk away. No guilt. No explanation.

✓ Recognising my triggers – Certain people, places, and habits no longer have access to me. I don't need to prove anything by putting myself in situations that compromise my growth.

✓ Honouring rest – I used to see stillness as weakness. Now I know it's where healing happens. Stillness used to feel like being trapped with my own thoughts. Now, it's a conscious act of recovery—for my mind, body, and nervous system.

✓ Processing emotions instead of suppressing them – I don't bottle things up any more, I feel them. I write. I speak. I allow them to pass through instead of lodging themselves in my body.

✓ Trusting myself again – I no longer override my gut instinct to make others comfortable. My intuition saved me. Now, I listen to it.

The biggest difference now is simple: I am in control. Life doesn't just happen to me any more—I respond, act, and choose every day. And that's the real freedom.

———

The Hardest Truth: Some People Only Valued Me When I Was Useful to Them

One of the most painful lessons I had to learn in this journey is this: Not everyone claps when you start healing.

Some people only liked the broken version of me. The version who was always available. Always saying yes. Always fixing, listening, giving—no matter the cost to myself. But when I started setting boundaries? Saying no? Choosing myself? The silence was deafening.

I watched people fade away. Messages stopped. Invitations vanished. Some people who constantly leaned on me during their lowest moments, disappeared as soon as I stopped playing the rescuer. That hurt—but it brought clarity.

Because real love isn't conditional. Real friends don't disappear when you get healthier.

Now, I don't chase connection—I allow it. If someone's love is transactional, they're not part of my future. And I'm okay with that.

―――

Amber: My Anchor in Transformation

Amber has been my mirror, my anchor, my home.

She loved me when I was hard to love. She stood by me when I was slipping, spiralling, self-destructing—but she never enabled me. She challenged me. She held space for me and held me accountable.

There was a moment, early on, when I started facing life more consciously—cutting back, making deliberate choices, refusing to numb out the way I used to. I wasn't fully sober, not yet. But I was no longer running. No longer escaping. And in one of those early moments when cravings crept in, when the pull to disconnect felt strong, she didn't shame me. She sat beside me. Held my hand. Reminded me why I was doing this—and who I was choosing to become.

Her presence, calm and non-judgmental, reminded me of what real love looks like.

She could've walked. And I wouldn't have blamed her. But she stayed.

Because of her, I learned what it means to be seen. To be loved for who I am—not who I pretend to be.

Now, I show up for her fully. Present. Sober. Honest. Aware. We've rebuilt everything on emotional safety, respect, and grounded, real love.

I will never take that for granted again.

The Biggest Lesson: Happiness Was Always There

For years, I believed happiness was something to chase. Something outside myself. I thought it was found in parties, people, approval, money, status. But none of it stuck. Because none of it came from within.

Now I understand:

- Happiness isn't found in a bottle, a person, or a bank balance.
- It lives inside you.
- It always has.

The joy I feel today isn't loud or chaotic, it's quiet. Stable. A warm glow inside instead of a short-lived firework. The peace I used to crave through drinking? I've found it in stillness, in connection, in living fully present.

You attract peace when you become peace.

The Grounded Moments That Prove It's Real

Some of the most healing moments aren't dramatic. They're calm. Human. Present.

There was a weekend where Amber and I went to a concert — one of my favourite artists. She'd bought the tickets for Valentine's Day. The following weekend, we went to an intimate performance she'd chosen — something more reflective and calming. We sat there, phones off, not speaking much — just being. Fully immersed. Fully there.

No distractions. No chaos. Just presence.

It wasn't just a night out—it was a moment of pure clarity. We were connected. Still. Fulfilled. And it hit me: this is what life is supposed to feel like.

Not forced. Not performative. Just real.

———

If I Could Tell My Past Self One Thing

If I could go back to that broken, spiralling version of me lying in bed—dissociated, lost—I'd whisper:

💬 "This isn't the end. It's the beginning."

💬 "You're not too far gone. You're not broken beyond repair. You are becoming."

💬 "You already have everything inside you that you're searching for."

💬 "You don't need to prove your worth. You just need to return to it."

And I'd remind him: One day, you'll write this book. One day, you'll help others heal. One day, you'll look in the mirror and finally smile with pride—not performance.

———

Stepping Into Your New Life

Questions to Reflect On:

- What boundaries have you been avoiding because you're afraid of disappointing others?
- What does peace look like for you—and are you chasing it externally or creating it internally?
- Who supports your growth—and who fades away when you start changing?
- What small acts can you commit to this week to honour your healing?
- What version of you needs to be released so that the real you can rise?

Insight

Stepping into your new life doesn't mean everything will be perfect. It means you've chosen truth over performance, peace over chaos, and self-respect over self-abandonment. That's real freedom.

Final Thoughts—This Is Just the Start

I've built a life I love—not because it's perfect, but because it's mine. A life of calm mornings, real love, purpose-driven work, and presence. A life built on truth.

And I'm still learning. Still growing. Still climbing.

But now? I'm doing it from clarity, not confusion. From peace, not panic.

And if you're reading this—you can too.

You don't need to wait. You don't need to have it all figured out.

You just need to start. Because this life? The one you dream about? It's already inside you.

You just have to choose it.

Chapter 7: Manifestation, Reprogramming, and Building a New Reality

At some point, a shift happened in my life. A moment when I realised I wasn't just trapped in cycles—I was actively creating them.

It wasn't just life happening to me. I was making decisions—sometimes unconsciously—that kept me locked in old patterns. The self-destruction, the people-pleasing, the chaos, the highs and crashes... I wasn't just a victim of my circumstances. I was participating in them.

And that meant I had the power to change them.

For years, I'd told myself I was trying. "I'm working on it," I'd say. But really, I was chipping away at the surface while avoiding the foundation. Real change required something deeper.

It meant completely rewiring how I thought, how I reacted, how I saw myself.

And the first step? I stopped living on autopilot.

From Calm to Conscious Creation

That stillness I talked about in the last chapter—the quiet moments with Amber, the deep presence, the peace? That didn't just mark the end of chaos. It laid the foundation for this next phase.

Because once you find calm, you finally have the space to see what's underneath.

It's like your nervous system softens, your inner world gets quieter, and you realise: I'm not broken. I'm just patterned. And I can change the pattern.

The Power of Reprogramming Your Mind

I started questioning everything.

Before I reacted, I asked myself:

- Does this serve me?
- Does this align with who I want to be?
- Is this autopilot or intention?

This simple practice changed everything. Because when you become aware of your default thoughts, behaviours, and emotional reactions, you give yourself the power to choose something new.

Ask Yourself:

What are the thought loops or emotional reactions that keep repeating in my life?

Where am I still running a story that no longer serves me?

I had to let go of so much:

- Chasing external validation.
- Playing the fixer.
- Keeping people around just to feel needed.

- Being "the strong one" at the expense of my own needs.

I created a new baseline—one that said: "My energy is mine. My worth is not up for debate. I don't have to prove anything to be loved."

Rituals That Rewired Me

Reprogramming didn't just happen in my head. It happened through action.

Here are a few of the daily rituals that helped shift my reality:

- I journaled every morning—even if it was messy or short.
- I paused before every major decision and asked myself, "Does this pull me back into old cycles, or move me forward?"
- I visualised the highest version of myself and tried to act like him—even before I felt like him.
- I meditated, even if I struggled with stillness. Just sitting changed things.
- I wrote letters to my inner child. To my future self.

Each of these grounded me. Anchored me. Made me more me.

Where Energy Goes, Energy Flows

I stopped pouring energy into people and places that couldn't hold it. I stopped chasing. Stopped fixing.

Stopped explaining myself to those who only heard me when I was broken.

Instead, I redirected that energy inward. And I felt stronger. Clearer. Lighter.

If you're in that place now—pouring all your energy into something that never gives back—ask yourself: What would happen if I took all that energy and gave it to myself instead?

A Human Moment – Life Still Happens

Let me be real. Even now, with all the growth and clarity, life still throws shit at me.

Lately, I've been navigating massive change—personally and professionally. Juggling multiple businesses, preparing to leave full-time work, fighting battles for my family's wellbeing, writing this book, holding space for others, and trying not to lose myself in the process.

And some days, I feel flat. Stretched thin. Overwhelmed.

But here's the difference: I deal with it—I don't run from it. I face it head-on, with clarity, strength, and intention.

And every time I do, I build more trust within myself. This is what healing actually looks like. Not perfection—but presence.

You're still going to have days that knock you sideways. But when you're rooted in self-trust, you stop spiralling. You handle it. You return to your centre.

That's power.

The Dream That Changed Everything

One night, I had a dream I'll never forget. I was inside a cage, deep inside a dark cave. The air was cold. The light was barely there. The walls were stone—damp, echoing with everything I'd buried. But the cage door? It was already open.

In my hand was a key. One I'd been holding the whole time. That moment hit me like a lightning bolt: I was never really trapped, I just believed I was.

When I woke up, I knew that image had to be the back cover of this book. Because it is the story.

That's all recovery is: the moment you realise the lock was never real. And the exit? It's right in front of you.

This is Where Manifestation Gets Real

You don't manifest what you want. You manifest who you are. So I became the version of me I'd been waiting for. And things started shifting. Fast. Not because of magic—but because I aligned with what I deserved.

Let Go of the Old Story

Here are some truths that might hurt at first—but will free you:

- You are not your past.
- You are not your mistakes.
- You are not your trauma.

- You are who you choose to be now.

Write a letter to your past self. To your inner child. To the version of you who didn't know better.

Tell them: "Thank you. But I've got it from here."

This is where you stop coping—and start creating.

Your Turn – Reflect, Rewire, Reclaim

Get your journal. Take your time. Go deep.

Write these out. Be honest:

- What beliefs about yourself are you ready to release?
- Where are you still living on autopilot?
- To whom or what are you giving energy that drains you?
- What version of yourself are you manifesting with your actions right now?
- What would it look like to show up as your highest self today—even in one small way?

🗝 Bonus exercise: Write a letter to your future self.

Describe who you are, how you feel, what you've created, and how you got there. Read it aloud. Believe it. Then become it.

Final Thoughts – The Door Was Always Open

If you've been waiting for a sign, this is it. You're not stuck. You're not trapped. You've been holding the key all along. The chaos you're in? It's not your identity. The cage? It was never locked.

And you? You're already walking out of it. One choice. One shift. One decision at a time.

You're not just healing any more. You're building. You're becoming.

And it's already happening—right now.

Chapter 8: Rewiring Your Identity and Creating Real Change

Real change doesn't come from a single breakthrough, it comes from the small, uncomfortable, conscious choices you make every single day. It's not just walking out of the cage—it's making sure you don't walk back in.

Clarity is powerful. But clarity without action? That's just another excuse to stay the same.

For years, I told myself I was changing. Cutting down. "Doing the work." But the truth? I was still leaving the door open for chaos. Still chasing control instead of creating discipline. Still convincing myself that surviving was the same thing as healing.

The real shift happened when I took full ownership. Of every decision. Every emotion. Every consequence. And I started asking myself, constantly:

- Does this serve me?
- Does this serve Amber and my family?
- Is this going to set me back?

Those questions became my daily compass. And that's when everything started to shift—from an identity built on survival… to one built on self-mastery.

———

Letting Go of Who I Thought I Had to Be

I used to believe I had to be the loud one. The fun one. The one who made everyone else feel better, even if I was falling apart inside.

I thought if I wasn't being seen, I wasn't being valued. That if I wasn't entertaining, I wasn't enough. That chaos was the price of connection.

But that version of me wasn't my truth.

It was a performance. A coping mechanism. An identity stitched together from trauma and noise.

Rewiring meant unlearning everything I thought made me worthy.

☑ I am not loveable only when I'm useful.

☑ I am not stronger when I keep it all in.

☑ I do not need chaos to feel alive.

Real connection doesn't come from performance. It comes from presence.

Micro-Moment: The Day I Stopped Trying to Convince People

One of the biggest shifts happened in a quiet moment. I was trying to explain something deeply personal to someone—something I thought they'd understand. But I could tell they weren't really listening. They were nodding, half-engaged, already forming their reply.

The old me would've pushed harder. Tried to make them understand. Win them over. Please them.

But something inside me said, "Stop talking." Not out of bitterness—but out of clarity. If someone isn't listening, stop talking.

That's energy I used to waste. Not any more. I don't chase being understood. I protect my peace. Because there are people who will lean in, who will get it, who are ready. I speak to them now.

———

The Habits That Helped Me Rewire

You don't think your way into a new identity, you act your way there.

Here's what grounded me:

- Meditation – Not perfection. Just stillness. Sitting with myself, even when it was uncomfortable.

- Gratitude – Every night: Three things, no matter how small. It rewired my brain from scarcity to presence.

- The Pause – One breath between trigger and reaction. That pause saved relationships, days, and my own peace more times than I can count.

- Energy Boundaries – I stopped letting draining people rent space in my mind. If it costs peace, it's too expensive.

The Rise of Emotional Maturity

I don't drown in my emotions any more. I don't suppress them or pretend they're not there. Now I check in with myself daily:

- "How am I feeling right now?"
- "What is this emotion trying to tell me?"

And if something's coming up—I sit with it. I honour it. I speak about it.

I used to believe I had to do everything alone. That vulnerability was weakness. That emotions were something to avoid.

Now? I speak to people I trust. I lean on support. I allow myself to be held when I need it. And that's not weakness—that's strength. That's clarity.

A Hard Truth: I Used to Be Fickle

I used to hate that trait in other people—fickleness, inconsistency, empty promises. But when I reflected deeper, I realised I'd been like that too. Not out of malice—but out of survival.

I wasn't pausing. I wasn't thinking. I was people-pleasing, scrambling to be liked, avoiding discomfort. But that went against my values. That's not who I truly am.

Now, I pause and ask: Does this align with who I want to be? Am I choosing clarity—or comfort?

I'm not flaky any more. I'm focused. Aligned. When I say something—I mean it.

The "Let Them" Theory Changed Everything

Mel Robbins' "Let Them" theory hit me like a brick. Let them ignore you. Let them not support you. Let them distance themselves when you grow. It's not rejection. It's redirection.

You stop trying to control other people's behaviour—and you start reclaiming your energy. The people who are meant for you will never need to be convinced.

The Power of Alignment

Manifestation isn't magic, it's alignment. It's living in the energy of who you say you want to be—even before the world reflects it back to you.

- I stopped proving and started becoming.
- I stopped chasing and started choosing.
- I stopped waiting and started acting.

And slowly, everything around me began to mirror who I was becoming.

The right people showed up. The right opportunities flowed. Not because I forced it—but because I was finally ready to receive it.

Mini Crash Moments – But Now I Deal With Them

Let's be real. Life didn't magically become smooth.

Even now, things hit me hard—stress, uncertainty, difficult choices. There were weeks when it felt like the universe was throwing everything at me: personal stress, career pressure, emotional exhaustion.

But I handled it differently. I didn't spiral. I didn't numb. I didn't run. I faced it. I paused. I breathed. I made space.

Every time I showed up for myself, I built trust with myself. That's self-mastery. Not being perfect—but being present. Being honest, and staying the course even when things get heavy.

That's what rewiring looks like.

Micro-Moment: Realising I'd Never Put Myself First

Another moment that changed me came during a conversation when someone asked me, "What do you want?"

I couldn't answer. Not straight away.

I'd spent so long defining myself by what others needed from me—attention, energy, help, validation—I'd completely lost sight of who I actually was.

That's when I knew: I had to start choosing me. Not just for peace. Not just to set boundaries. But because I didn't even know who I was any more.

What do I like?

What do I want to do with my life?

What are my values—mine, not inherited or shaped to fit in?

I wasn't just choosing myself—I was trying to find myself.

And once I started living for that—not for approval, not for acceptance, not for applause, but for truth—everything changed.

Who Are You Becoming?

Questions to Reflect On:

Pause here. Grab your journal. Take a breath. Reflect.

- What habits or people are still tied to your old identity?

- Where are you still people-pleasing or performing?
- What do you need to let go of to become who you're meant to be?
- Who are you when you're not performing, coping, or escaping?
- What small habit could you commit to daily that aligns with the version of you who you want to become?

Optional Exercise

Write a letter to your inner child, your past self, or your future self. Say the things they needed to hear. Let them know you're showing up now. That you're not abandoning them again.

Final Thoughts: Change Is Who You Are Now

This isn't just something you're working on. This is who you are now.

You're not going backwards. You're not spiralling. You're building. One aligned choice at a time. One honest pause. One boundary. One breath.

You've already stepped through the open cage door.

Now you're learning how to fly.

Chapter 9: Becoming Who I Was Always Meant To Be

It's rarely comfortable when you start becoming who you're truly meant to be. It demands honesty, vulnerability, and courage in equal measure. It's about standing in front of a mirror and seeing past your reflection—deeper, into the person hiding beneath the mask you've worn for so long. For me, that mirror moment came when I realised I was no longer running from something. I was finally running towards something.

For years, I'd been caught in chaos. An endless cycle of numbing myself, losing myself, and desperately trying to find myself again. But as the fog cleared, the real me started to emerge—not overnight, but slowly, painfully, beautifully. I stopped asking, "Who am I supposed to be?" and started embracing who I actually was: ambitious, driven, intuitive, emotionally deep, and yes—flawed. But always willing to learn, heal, and grow.

And then, something I never expected started to happen.

Amber, my mum, dad, and sister noticed the shift. Their eyes no longer portrayed worry or cautious hope—but pride. Real, genuine pride. When they said they were proud of me, I didn't just hear it, I felt it. I believed it—not just in my head, but deep in my soul. Those moments meant everything. It was the first time I truly allowed their love and belief to land.

But becoming who you're meant to be isn't just about how others see you, it's about how you see yourself—and the boundaries you begin to honour.

From Overgiver to Energy Protector

I used to be the helper. Always available. Always giving. Even when I had nothing left. I didn't know how to value myself unless I was useful to others.

And the truth is—most people only valued me when I was useful to them.

It hit hard when I realised no one really checked in unless I was joining their chaos or fixing their mess. But learning to say "no"—without guilt—was revolutionary. Learning to walk away from the people who only called when they needed something was one of the deepest acts of self-respect I'd ever taken.

The quiet that followed felt uncomfortable at first. Lonely, even.

But eventually, that quiet turned into peace. My circle got smaller. Stronger. More intentional. And I was no longer performing for connection—I was inviting it from alignment.

Amber: The Light That Never Left

Throughout all of this, Amber remained my constant. The one who stood beside me when I was lost, and who now stands beside me in the light. She never enabled me. She never tried to fix me. She just… stayed. She saw me—really saw me—when I couldn't even see myself.

She held space for my growth and called me out when I started slipping. She showed me that real love is both soft and strong. Her presence is the reason I believe in unconditional love. And now? I get to show up for her. Fully. Grounded. Sober. Loving. Present.

We build our life together now on truth, mutual respect, and peace. And I will never take that for granted.

The Hard Mirror of Family & Legacy

My family's always known I had ambition, but for a long time, that ambition looked like chaos—like I was always chasing something, never still, never grounded.

It used to sting when people said, "You're always chasing something else." But now I know—that fire in me, the hunger, the drive—that's what saved me. That ambition pulled me from the darkest places. That relentless spirit is what allowed me to build, transform, and become.

Reflecting on my mam, I can see now that the same traits live in her too. Her constant movement, her drive, her fierce love—maybe those were her ways of coping as well. And when I look at that now, I don't judge it. I get it. I see it with compassion. It's helped me understand her more deeply than I ever did before.

My mam, my dad, and my sister — they are the foundation. Of love. Of resilience. Of strength. They've taught me more than they probably realise. They are, without doubt, the strongest people I know.

A Moment That Changed Everything

One of the hardest, most confronting moments came through my sister's battle with depression. A time when we almost lost her. That kind of fear—raw, helpless, life-or-death—etched something permanent into me.

Being by her side through that time changed something in me. It brought us even closer. Her survival became a second chance for all of us—a reminder to hold each other tighter, speak more honestly, and never take a heartbeat for granted.

This journey isn't just about me. It's about all of us.

Micro-Moments of Becoming

The big shifts didn't just happen in therapy or through huge breakthroughs—they happened in the quiet choices. The small rewires.

Like when I stopped drowning in my emotions and started facing them.

I used to either bottle things up or let them explode. Now, I check in. I talk. I journal. I ask, "What is this emotion trying to tell me?" Because emotions aren't weaknesses—they're signals. They're your body's way of communicating.

And for the first time in my life, I don't try to handle everything alone.

I ask for help. I open up. I trust the people around me with my truth. Delegation, communication, vulnerability—these were once terrifying to me. Now, they're part of my daily life.

And it's changed everything.

From People-Pleasing to Personal Power

I used to be so desperate for approval. I'd try to win people over, explain myself endlessly, convince them to see my side.

Now? If someone isn't listening—I stop talking. That one shift has saved me hours of emotional energy.

There's no more trying to prove myself to the wrong people. No more dancing for the crumbs of validation. No more chasing flaky connections.

I used to hate fickleness in others—and deep down, it was because I recognised it in myself. That old version of me, shaped by survival and people-pleasing, was inconsistent. Reactive. Trying to be everything to everyone.

Now? I choose values over validation, stillness over scrambling. I ask: "Does this serve me? Does this serve the life I'm building?"

If not—it's a no.

The New Me Isn't Perfect—But He's Whole

This version of me still has bad days. Still gets overwhelmed. Still questions things sometimes.

But I'm no longer running. I'm no longer hiding. I'm no longer abandoning myself.

And the pride I feel? It's internal. Rooted. Real.

To the version of me who didn't know how to stop performing…

I see you. The one who didn't feel heard, so he turned up the volume. The one who kept giving, hoping someone would finally ask if he was okay. The one who didn't know he was already worthy.

Thank you for surviving.

But I've got it from here.

―――――

To you—yes, you, reading this...

You don't have to keep proving yourself to people who were never tried to understand you. You don't have to shrink yourself to fit into versions of the past.

You're allowed to want more. You're allowed to evolve. It's safe to change. It's safe to let go of what no longer fits. It's safe to become the version of you who no longer doubts their worth.

―――――

Final Thoughts: Becoming is a Choice

If you're reading this and wondering when it gets easier, here's the truth: It's not about easy—it's about true.

When you start living in alignment with your truth, it might not always be smooth—but it will be worth it.

You don't have to get it perfect, it just has to be honest. You already know who you are deep down. It's time to stop doubting and start deciding.

You're not becoming someone else. You're becoming who you were always meant to be.

Chapter 10: Living the Truth, Not Just Speaking It

There comes a point in your journey when you stop talking about change and just become it.

It's quiet. Not dramatic. Not filled with announcements or social media declarations. Just different. Real. Rooted.

This chapter isn't about breakthroughs or breakdowns. It's about embodiment—what happens when you stop trying to prove you've changed, and you start living like the person you always knew you could be.

I'm no longer searching for the path. I am the path.

When Truth Becomes Your Default

The old me wanted everyone to understand. I'd overexplain myself, try to prove I had good intentions, convince people I was still worth sticking with. I'd exhaust myself trying to be seen.

Now? I'm okay with being misunderstood. That's the cost of peace—letting people draw their own conclusions while you stay grounded in your own clarity.

There's a freedom that comes with letting go of the need to be liked, understood, or validated. I stopped just saying I'd changed—and started showing it in the way I move, the way I respond, the way I protect my energy.

The Power of Silence and Alignment

Not everything needs a response. Not every message needs a reply. Not every situation needs fixing.

The real strength is in silence—the pause before the reaction, the space between the trigger and the response.

Now, I ask myself:

- Does this require my energy?
- Does this conversation build anything?
- Is this reaction about them… or about something unhealed in me?

And most of the time, the answer is: let it go.

There's nothing to prove when you're already at peace with yourself.

One powerful realisation hit me like a brick: "If someone isn't listening, stop talking."

This one changed everything for me.

I used to chase people's understanding. I'd reword things, try again, try harder—especially if I cared about them. I thought if I just explained it better, they'd get it. But now?

I've learned that if someone isn't really listening—not just hearing the words, but open to understanding—then it's not worth the energy.

There's a quote by Jordan Peterson that summed it up perfectly, and it stuck with me:

"If people are not listening to you, stop talking to them... If you have things to say, say them, but find people who will listen... Because you're devaluing what you have to say by offering it to an audience that does nothing but reject it."

That shifted something in me.

You don't have to scream your truth. Just live it. The right people will feel it—without you needing to perform or beg to be understood.

From People-Pleasing to Peacekeeping

The old me hated the idea of disappointing anyone. I'd say yes when I wanted to say no. I'd stretch myself thin, betraying my own needs just to keep the peace.

But that wasn't peace—it was performance. And it cost me myself.

Now, I keep the peace within me. I'm no longer available for fickleness, for half-hearted friendships, or for being anyone's emotional caretaker.

If someone disappears when I stop giving—good. That was never connection. That was convenience.

One of the Biggest Emotional Shifts

I no longer drown in my emotions or run from them. I feel them.

I check in with myself. If I'm anxious, angry, flat, or overwhelmed—it's a signal, not a punishment.

Now, instead of shoving it down or numbing it out, I sit with it.

I journal. I speak to Amber. I reach out to people I trust. I no longer carry everything on my own.

I thought vulnerability made me weak. But it's made me indestructible.

Because when you stop bottling everything up, when you start allowing yourself to be human—you take your power back.

Practical Rituals I Live By Now

- Morning silence – 10 minutes of no phone, no noise, just presence.

- Midday check-ins – "How am I feeling? What do I need?"

- Evening reflection – wins, triggers, gratitude, and adjustments.
- The pause – before replying, before reacting, before spiralling.
- Energy audit – "Did this lift me or drain me?" If it drains me more than twice—it's gone.

Questions to Reflect On:

Ask yourself:

- Where am I still overexplaining my truth?
- What conversations am I having out of guilt, not alignment?
- Where am I performing to find peace instead of creating it?
- What would living my truth actually look like in my daily life?

You don't need to be louder. You just need to be truer.

Legacy, Impact, and What's Next

This book isn't just a story—it's a statement. It's proof that we're allowed to grow, change, and heal—and still be flawed, still be learning, still be figuring it out.

I don't have it all sorted. But I know who I am. I know what matters. And I'm building my life around that.

From Breaking Free, to now living freely—that's the legacy.

And the best part? You don't have to wait for permission. You can start living yours today.

Final Thoughts: Truth Lived > Truth Spoken

You can read all the books. Say all the right words. Post all the quotes. But until you embody the truth… nothing changes.

This chapter isn't about performance. It's about presence.

So, start small. One truth. One decision. One moment of choosing alignment over approval. Then do it again tomorrow.

And soon, you'll realise: You don't have to say it any more. They'll just feel it.

Chapter 11: The Journey Continues

Breaking free isn't a destination—it's a lifelong journey.

I used to believe that once I had overcome the worst parts of myself, life would settle into ease. But I've learned something deeper—breaking free is a daily decision, a conscious commitment to keep choosing growth, truth, and self-respect... even when it's hard.

Even now, old patterns still whisper to me. Triggers still try to test me. But the difference is, I see them now. And I respond, I don't react.

I don't spiral like I used to. I don't run. I don't become numb.

I breathe. I pause. I move through it.

This chapter of the journey hasn't been without its challenges. If anything, it's brought more responsibility, more awareness, more pressure to stay aligned. But that's where real freedom lives—in showing up differently when life doesn't go to plan.

Choosing the Higher Path When It's Hard

Lately, life hasn't exactly gone easy on me.

Between managing multiple businesses, planning to leave my job, and carrying the emotional weight of everything I'm building—I felt the pressure rising.

The old me would've cracked. He would've escaped, lashed out, spiralled, or used chaos as a coping mechanism. He would've convinced himself he deserved to fall apart.

But I didn't. I paused. I breathed.

I reminded myself: how I respond now is the proof of how far I've come. So I stayed grounded. I faced it. I moved forward.

That moment became a mirror—not just reflecting who I used to be, but showing me the man I've become.

Supporting Others Without Losing Myself

There's something else I've learned lately—something massive.

You can't help people by losing yourself.

I used to think love meant giving everything. Being the one who fixed it, carried it, rescued them, stayed up all night pouring from a dry cup.

But now I see the difference. Support doesn't mean self-sacrifice. Real love doesn't mean abandoning yourself for someone else. You can hold space for someone without drowning in their storm.

Now, I help from clarity—not chaos. I've learned to say, "I'm here with you" rather than "Let me carry it all."

And that shift? That boundary?

It's saved me. It's saved relationships. It's given me the strength to be there—without burning out.

Watching Others Shift Because of Your Growth

One of the most powerful things that's happened lately has been watching others begin to shift—just by witnessing my journey.

I haven't forced anything. I haven't preached.

I've just stayed consistent. Honest. Imperfect, but real.

And now I see it. In how someone I love speaks differently about their emotions. In how a friend started setting boundaries they never dared to before. In how people reach out—not because I'm a crutch—but because they trust the version of me who's grounded now.

Healing ripples.

When you change, others feel it. And when you lead with truth instead of ego… people notice. This work matters.

And those small moments—those changes in others—they remind me why I keep showing up.

Seeing Myself Through My Family's Eyes

Amber felt the shift. And so did my mum, my dad, and my sister. The way they looked at me changed. It wasn't just relief—it was pride. Like they weren't just hoping I'd be okay any more... they *knew* I was.

They've always believed in me. But now? Now they trust who I am. And more importantly, so do I.

I'm not "too much." I'm driven. I'm hungry. I'm here to do something with this life.

That fire in my belly? It saved me.

———

Letting Go of Those Who Only Liked the Old Me

Some people only liked me when I was useful. When I said yes to everything. When I joined in the chaos. When I was self-abandoning in the name of "fun".

But when I started changing? When I set boundaries? When I stopped showing up just to keep the peace? They disappeared.

And yeah—it hurt. At first, it felt like rejection. But now I see it for what it was: redirection.

———

I Don't Run From Emotions Any More

This one's huge.

I used to drown in emotions. Or worse—run from them. Push them down. Bottle them up. Numb them out.

Now? I face them. If I feel something, I listen. I sit with it. I journal. I reflect. I ask: What is this emotion trying to tell me? What do I need right now?

I've learned emotions aren't weaknesses. They're signals. They're feedback. And if you actually pay attention, they become your greatest compass.

And for the first time in my life—I don't feel like I have to carry everything alone.

I talk. To people I trust. To people who see me. To people who want to hold space, not fix me.

That's new. That's powerful.

And that's the biggest shift of all.

Final Thoughts: The Journey Is Still Ongoing

This chapter of my life isn't perfect. There are still moments when I feel flat. When I feel tired. When everything I'm building feels overwhelming.

But now, I know how to hold both. The expansion and the exhaustion. The ambition and the stillness.

This is the beauty of the middle. You're not who you were. You're not quite who you're becoming. But you're here. Alive. Present. Growing.

And that's enough.

Questions to Reflect On:

Before we move on, I want to leave you with a few questions. You don't have to have all the answers. But you do have to be honest.

- What's testing you right now—and how can you choose the higher path?
- Are you supporting others from clarity or from chaos?
- Who around you is shifting because you've shown them a different way?
- What emotion have you been avoiding that's quietly asking for your attention?
- Where are you still giving your energy to people who don't deserve it?

You don't need to be perfect. You just need to be present. Keep going.

You're not behind. You're not late. You're becoming.

And trust me—the next version of you is going to blow your mind.

Chapter 12: This Is Just the Beginning

I used to think healing had an endpoint. That if I just worked hard enough, I'd arrive—clean, healed, whole. That I'd hit some magical moment where I could say, "I made it."

But the truth? You never really arrive.

Because this work isn't about reaching some perfect version of yourself, it's about becoming, again and again. Choosing, again and again. Breaking free, again and again. And that's the most beautiful thing about it.

Because freedom isn't something you find—it's something you become.

The Truth About Healing

Healing isn't neat. It's not a straight line. It's not a sunrise after the storm. Sometimes, it is the storm.

Sometimes it's crying in the middle of a calm week because a memory surfaces that you thought you had buried.

Sometimes it's choosing not to react when your old self would've exploded.

Sometimes it's walking away from someone you love because their energy no longer aligns.

Sometimes it's just getting through the day—and calling that a win.

I've learned that healing is a practice. It's a choice. A muscle. A frequency. It's learning to hold duality—joy and grief, strength and softness, clarity and confusion—all in the same breath. And still choosing to keep going.

―――

Who You Are Now

You've come this far. Through every reflection. Every journal prompt. Every hard truth that hit you in the chest.

You've sat with discomfort. You've walked through old memories. You've faced things most people spend their lives avoiding.

And here you are. Not fixed. Not perfect. But awake.

You're not who you were at the beginning of this book. You're not lost. You're not broken. You're not too far gone. You are becoming—in real time.

This version of you is the result of every decision you've made to show up when it was easier not to. Every pause before a reaction. Every breath instead of a bottle. Every boundary you held. Every emotion you let rise instead of running.

And I hope you see that.

―――

What Comes Next?

You're not meant to stay the same, you're meant to evolve. So if you feel the pull to change again six months from now—let yourself. If you feel called to leave something behind again—trust that call. If you're pulled back into old patterns—meet yourself with love, not shame. You're still human.

The real power lies in self-awareness and in your ability to return to yourself over and over. And the path ahead? It's yours to shape.

There is no one "right" way. There is only your way—guided by your truth, your integrity, your alignment.

And if you ever forget? Return to this moment. Return to yourself. Come back home.

―――

From Chaos to Clarity—For Good

The person writing this now is not the person who began this journey. I'm calmer. More grounded. More in love with my life, my wife, my purpose.

I speak to myself with respect. I stand in my truth. I've stopped performing. I've stopped running. I've stopped abandoning myself to make others comfortable.

And you know what? It's peaceful here. Not perfect. Not without its challenges. But peaceful in the way I never thought possible. Because I've created safety within myself. And now, I don't seek it elsewhere.

———

What I Know Now

You do not need to prove your worth. You do not need to stay where you're not seen. You do not need to perform your pain or water down your truth.

You are worthy—as you are. Not when you're fully healed. Not when your past is behind you. Not when you finally "get it together".

Now. Right here. Right now.

You are enough. And everything you need to live the life you want? It's already inside you.

———

Your Invitation

So as you close this book, I want to leave you with one final task.

Don't write another letter. **Write a declaration.**

Not to your past self. Not to your future self. To the you standing here, right now.

Write down what you're no longer willing to tolerate.

Write down what you're choosing instead.

Write down what you know to be true about yourself—whether the world sees it yet or not.

Make it bold. Make it honest. Make it yours.

Because this isn't the end. It's your beginning.

Your next chapter starts now.

———

Final Words

To everyone who's walked this journey with me, who's seen themselves in these pages—thank you.

To my wife, Amber—this book is for you. Your love was the anchor that steadied me in every storm. You showed me what real partnership, real presence, real devotion looks like. You loved me at my lowest and stayed with me as I climbed.

You are the soul I never saw coming, but always needed.

To you, the reader—wherever you are right now. Choose yourself. Even when it's hard—especially when it's hard.

Show up. Breathe through it. Write your next page with intention.

You've already begun.

And remember this always: One decision can change everything.

Now it's your turn. Break free. Choose clarity. And live like the person you were always meant to be.

Chapter 13: Your Turn to Break Free

If you're here—reading this final chapter—it means you've stayed with yourself through every word. Through the heavy parts. Through the quiet parts. Through the storm and the stillness. And that alone? That's powerful.

It means you showed up. For the first time in a long time—or maybe for the first time ever—you chose to sit with the truth instead of running from it. You leaned in, even when it hurt.

So before we go any further, let me say this clearly: **I'm proud of you.**

Because this journey isn't easy. It's not neat or linear. It doesn't come with a manual or a guarantee. But it does come with this truth: **You're not too far gone. You're not broken. And your story is not over.**

This Book Was Never Just About Me

Yes, these pages carried my story. My breakdown. My spiral. My reckoning. But every word was written with *you* in mind. The one who's tired of performing. The one who's exhausted by chaos. The one who keeps saying, *"I'm fine"*—but feels like they're falling apart.

This wasn't just my story. It's a mirror. A conversation. A lifeline.

Because deep down, I know what you might still be wondering: **"Is change really possible for me?"**

And here's the answer: **Yes.** But only if you choose it.

Where You Go From Here

Let's get one thing straight: transformation doesn't come with fireworks.

It's not some grand, dramatic shift. It's the quiet, uncomfortable, *consistent* choices you make when no one's watching.

It's the decision to:

- Leave the party early instead of spiralling.
- Sit with discomfort instead of numbing it.
- Tell the truth instead of performing.
- Show up for yourself the way you show up for everyone else.

It's not glamorous. But it's real.

And over time? **It changes everything.**

The Truth You Already Know

You can't keep living the same story and expect a different ending.

If your life has been built on performance, chaos, guilt, or survival, it's okay to want more. In fact, it's essential. You weren't born to suffer through your days and call it normal.

You were born to:

- Live present—not just survive.
- Feel peace—not just avoid pain.
- Be seen—not just tolerated.

You're not here to earn your worth. **You already have it.**

So stop shrinking. Stop apologising for needing more. Stop betraying yourself just to keep others comfortable.

Start Where You Are

You don't need to map out the rest of your life right now. You don't need to fix everything overnight. You just need to choose today.

Choose one small thing:

- Drink a glass of water and breathe deeply.
- Say no when you mean it.
- Rest without guilt.
- Text the friend who truly sees you.
- Delete the app that keeps pulling you into spirals.

These choices might not look like much from the outside. But from the inside? **They're everything.**

You Will Fall. But You'll Rise Faster

There will be days you slip. Days when the numbness calls louder than your truth. Days when you question whether you're really changing at all. That's normal.

But now? Now you know how to get back up. You know how to pause instead of spiral. You know what your triggers feel like. You know the difference between connection and chaos.

And most importantly? **You know you're worth saving.** Over and over again.

Your Truth Deserves Space

Questions to Reflect On:

Grab your journal or a scrap of paper. These questions are for you and you alone.

Be honest. Be raw. Be gentle.

- What cycle am I ready to break for good?
- What story have I been telling myself that it's time to let go of?
- What version of myself have I outgrown—and why am I still holding on to it?
- Who supports my healing—and who only loved the broken version of me?
- What would it feel like to live without the mask?

There's no "right" answer. Just the real one—and that's enough.

Final Affirmations: I Am Breaking Free

Say these aloud. Write them down. Let them echo through the parts of you still healing:

- I am not broken—I was surviving.
- I do not need to earn rest, love, or peace.
- I am allowed to say no.
- I am allowed to walk away.
- I am allowed to feel joy, even after pain.
- I am no longer available for chaos.
- I am safe to feel.
- I am ready to rise.
- I am choosing myself.
- **I am breaking free.**

Final Words

This isn't the end. This is your beginning. This is where you rise. This is where you come home to yourself.

And when you look back on this chapter months or years from now, you won't see breakdown.

You'll see breakthrough. From chaos to clarity. From spiralling to stillness. From surviving to becoming.

This is the moment you broke free.

Bonus Section: Letter to My Younger Self

Dear younger me,

You carried more than you should have—but it made you who you are.

You were just a kid trying to survive in a world that didn't know how to handle your sensitivity, your fire, your chaos. You were labelled *too much, too intense, too emotional*—and so you learned to shrink. To perform. To hide.

You spent years trying to be everything to everyone, and in the process, you forgot how to be anything to yourself. You chased highs to numb the lows. You mistook attention for love. You burned yourself out trying to be needed because it was the only time you felt wanted.

But here's what I want you to know—what I wish someone had told you back then: **You were never broken.**

The world just didn't know what to do with your bigness. Your emotions were not flaws. Your hunger for connection wasn't weakness. The fact that you felt things so deeply—that was your *gift*, not your curse.

I know there were nights you lay there thinking no one would ever understand the storm inside you. That you were too far gone. That maybe this was all there was.

But you were never too far gone.

Every single time you wanted to give up, you didn't. You got up. You showed up. You carried on.

That was never weakness. That was *strength*.

And I see you now—messy, lost, exhausted—and I want to wrap my arms around you and say: **You make it out.**

You grow into someone you're proud of. You learn how to sit with your emotions instead of drowning in them. You stop chasing people who don't choose you. You set boundaries that protect your peace. You love deeply, but you no longer abandon yourself to keep others close.

You find real connection. Real clarity. Real calm.

You finally understand that it's okay to be both healing and hurting, growing and grieving, rising and resting. That life isn't either/or—it's all of it, all at once.

And most importantly?

You become someone you never thought you could be.

I know you're scared. I know you feel like it's always going to be this hard. But it won't be.

One day, you'll look back and realise this was the moment everything started to shift. *Not because someone saved you.* But because *you chose to save yourself.*

I'm proud of you. I love you. And I promise—*your story isn't over. It's only just beginning.*

Keep going.

With love,

The version of you who finally broke free

— Nicky

Now It's Your Turn

Take a moment and write your own letter to your younger self. Say everything they needed to hear.

Tell them what you've survived, what you're learning, who you're becoming.

This is where healing begins.

Write it in your journal. Whisper it out loud. Or tear it up when you're done.

But whatever you do—let them know they were never alone.

You're here now.

And that changes everything.

Your Clarity Begins Here

Reflective Journal Page

You've read the story. You've felt the journey. Now it's your turn to write the next chapter of your own life.

Take a moment. Breathe. Reflect. Then write. These prompts are your beginning:

- What chapter hit you the hardest, and why?
- What pain are you finally ready to let go of?
- What chaos have you normalised that no longer serves you?
- What does your clarity look like?
- What's one decision you can make today that your future self will thank you for?
- Who are you becoming?

This isn't the end—it's your beginning.

You already hold the key.

Now step out of your cage.

Affirmations for the Journey

Read these aloud. Write them down. Keep them close.

These words are anchors when the waves rise.

- I am not broken. I am becoming.
- I release what no longer serves me.
- My past does not define my future.
- I choose clarity over chaos.
- I honour my emotions—they are signals, not weaknesses.

- I show up for myself—even when it's hard.
- I am allowed to be seen, loved, and supported.
- I trust my intuition. It knows the way.
- I attract people and energy that match my healing.
- I protect my peace like my life depends on it—because it does.
- I already hold the key to my freedom.
- I am rewriting my story, one conscious choice at a time.

🔑 Pick one. Write it on your mirror. Say it until you believe it.

———

Words That Help You Break Free – Recommended Reading

☑ **Can't Hurt Me – David Goggins**

 For extreme ownership, resilience, and building your mental edge.

☑ **Daring Greatly – Brené Brown**

 For learning how vulnerability becomes power—not weakness.

☑ **The Mountain Is You – Brianna Wiest**

 For understanding self-sabotage, emotional healing, and growth.

☑ **In the Realm of Hungry Ghosts –**

 For raw insight into addiction, trauma, and why we run from pain.

☑ **When the Body Says No – Dr. Gabor Maté**

 For the link between repressed emotions and chronic illness.

Resource Section – For When You Need It Most

If you're navigating your own healing journey—or simply need support—here are resources I trust and recommend.

You don't have to go it alone.

Support is real. Help exists. You're not broken—you're *becoming*.

📞 Crisis & Mental Health Hotlines

United Kingdom

- **Samaritans** – 116 123 (Free, 24/7)
- **SHOUT Crisis Text Line** – Text "SHOUT" to 85258
- **Mind** – 0300 123 3393 | www.mind.org.uk

United States

- **National Suicide Prevention Lifeline** – 988 or 1-800-273-TALK (8255)
- **Crisis Text Line** – Text "HOME" to 741741
- **NAMI** – 1-800-950-NAMI | www.nami.org

Australia

- **Lifeline** – 13 11 14
- **Beyond Blue** – 1300 22 4636 | www.beyondblue.org.au

———

Acknowledgements

To Amber—My wife. My anchor. My best friend. You are the heartbeat of this book.

Thank you for loving me when I was hard to love. For standing beside me in the darkness—and walking with me into the light.

Every page is for you. This book is ours.

To my family—Mam, Dad, my sister, my mother-in-law, my father-in-law, stepmother-in-law and every relative who's loved me through it all…

You've seen the worst, held space for the mess, and stayed when I didn't make it easy.

Thank you for never giving up on me.

This is the proof that I made it—and it's because of your love.

To the reader—Whether this book cracked you wide open or simply whispered, *"You're not alone",* thank you for reading it.

You held my truth—and now I hope it helps you hold yours.

You're not broken. You're becoming.

And the world needs who you're becoming.

About the Author

Nicky Re is an author, entrepreneur, and mental health advocate from the UK.

After years of battling addiction, emotional chaos, and self-destruction, Nicky rebuilt his life from the inside out.

Now, through his words, he helps others do the same.

His mission is to *make healing honest. To make clarity accessible. To help others break free — without shame.*

Nicky lives with his wife, Amber, and runs multiple ventures centred around healing, transformation, and emotional growth.

Breaking Free: A Journey from Chaos to Clarity is his debut book — and just the beginning.

———

Join the Movement

This isn't just a book. It's a movement.

A rising wave of people who are done pretending, done numbing, done hiding who they really are.

If this book spoke to you—if it cracked something open, helped you see yourself more clearly, or gave you a reason to believe again—then you're already part of this movement.

Now let the world know:

- → **Use the hashtag** #BreakingFreeBook on TikTok, Instagram, or Facebook.
- → **Share your favourite quotes, journal entries, or moments** that hit hardest.
- → **Tag me** @breakingfreebook so I can cheer you on.
- → **Leave a review** on Amazon or wherever you bought the book—your words might be the lifeline someone else needs.
- → **Visit** www.breakingfreebook.com to access free tools, updates, and community.

And if this book connected with you—if it resonated, supported you, or helped you reflect—**I'd genuinely love to hear from you.**

Whether you want to share your story, ask a question, or simply reach out—please feel free.

Email: hello@breakingfreebook.com

Socials: @breakingfreebook

Your journey matters.

Your voice matters.

This movement grows because of people like you.

Keep going. Keep healing. Keep showing up.

You are the proof that breaking free is possible.

www.ingramcontent.com/pod-product-compliance
Lightning Source LLC
Chambersburg PA
CBHW020427010526
44118CB00010B/453